BRYA
Real Vermonters
Address Book

DRAWINGS by HOWARD JOHNSON

© 1984 by Frank Bryan, William Mares,
and Howard Johnson
ALL RIGHTS RESERVED

For additional copies write to:

The New England Press, Inc.
P. O. Box 575
Shelburne, Vermont 05482

ISBN: 0–933050–24–0

PRINTED IN THE UNITED STATES OF AMERICA

BRYAN & MARES
Real Vermonters
Address Book

is for Ants and Antidotes.

Historian Charles Morrissey says life for many in Vermont "is a punishing, grueling ordeal of trying to scratch a living between a rock and a very hard place." Here is a list of Real Vermonter ways of counteracting the hardships of everyday survival in this most tough and most glorious state.

Ants At Vermont's Picnic	Antidote
Black flies	Long sleeves
Overgrown zucchini	Hogs
Freezing rain	"Stayin' tahome "[1]
Mud season	Sugaring
"Know-it-all" Flatlanders	Dead silence
Dry spells	Mowing hay[2]
Potato bugs	A thumb and a forefinger
Boredom	Flatlanders
Short woodpile in February	Ash[3]
Michael Jackson	On-off switch[4]
TV black-outs	Sleep
Woodchucks[5]	"00" buckshot
Leaf peepers	Raising prices
Broken axe handles	(Expletive deleted)
High taxes	Town Meeting
Cows that won't "settle"[6]	Auctions
Insomnia	Whippoorwills
John Easton	A full-time job

[1] This is also how Real Vermonters deal with dead batteries, traffic, and high gasoline prices.

[2] Flatlanders, of course, wash their cars or water their gardens.

[3] The all-forgiving firewood—it burns wet.

[4] It also works for Dick Snelling and Bernie Sanders.

[5] Garden variety.

[6] A Real Vermonterism for "conceive."

name • address • phone

A

_____
_____
_____ Zip_____
Phone: Home _____ Work_____
_____

_____
_____
_____ Zip_____
Phone: Home _____ Work_____
_____

_____
_____
_____ Zip_____
Phone: Home _____ Work_____
_____

_____
_____
_____ Zip_____
Phone: Home _____ Work_____
_____

_____
_____
_____ Zip_____
Phone: Home _____ Work_____
_____

_____
_____
_____ Zip_____
Phone: Home _____ Work_____
_____

_____
_____ Zip_____
Phone: Home _____ Work_____

A

name • address • phone

_____

_____
_____ Zip_____
Phone: Home _____ Work _____
_____

_____
_____ Zip_____
Phone: Home _____ Work _____
_____

_____
_____ Zip_____
Phone: Home _____ Work _____
_____

_____
_____ Zip_____
Phone: Home _____ Work _____
_____

_____
_____ Zip_____
Phone: Home _____ Work _____
_____

_____
_____ Zip_____
Phone: Home _____ Work _____
_____

_____ Zip_____
Phone: Home _____ Work _____

name • address • phone

A

_____
_____
_____ Zip_____
Phone: Home _____ Work _____

_____
_____
_____ Zip_____
Phone: Home _____ Work _____

_____
_____
_____ Zip_____
Phone: Home _____ Work _____

_____
_____
_____ Zip_____
Phone: Home _____ Work _____

_____
_____
_____ Zip_____
Phone: Home _____ Work _____

_____
_____
_____ Zip_____
Phone: Home _____ Work _____

_____
_____
_____ Zip_____
Phone: Home _____ Work _____

B is for Books, real and imagined.

The Real Vermonter's bookshelf should have . . .

- *Machine-gunning for Rabbits*
- *Teaching Your Wife to Change a Truck Tire*
- *Danvis Folks* by Rowland Robinson
- *Speaking from Vermont* by George Aiken
- *The Vermont Mind* by Jeff Danziger
- *The Joy of Snowmobiling*
- *Vermont Tradition* by Dorothy Canfield Fisher
- *Zen and the Art of Tractor Maintenance*
- *Contrary Country* by Ralph Nading Hill
- *Putting on Flatlanders for Fun and Profit*
- *Everything You Always Wanted to Know about New Hampshire but Forgot to Ask*
- *Reason the Only Oracle of Man* by Ethan Allen[1]
- *The Dick Snelling Workout Book*
- *North of Boston* by Robert Frost
- *The Sears, Roebuck and Co. Catalog*
- *The Sayings of Chairman Sanders*

[1]Known as "Ethan Allen's Bible," the full title of *Oracle* was a humdinger even for the 1780's: "Reason the Only Oracle of Man, or a Compenduous System of Natural Religion. Alternately Adorned with Confutations of a variety of Doctrines incompatable to it; Deduced from the most exalted Ideas which we are able to form of the Divine and Human Characters, and from the Universe in General."

name • address • phone   B

_____

_____
_____ Zip_____
Phone: Home _____ Work _____
_____

_____
_____ Zip_____
Phone: Home _____ Work _____
_____

_____
_____ Zip_____
Phone: Home _____ Work _____
_____

_____
_____ Zip_____
Phone: Home _____ Work _____
_____

_____
_____ Zip_____
Phone: Home _____ Work _____
_____

_____
_____ Zip_____
Phone: Home _____ Work _____
_____

_____
_____ Zip_____
Phone: Home _____ Work _____

B

name • address • phone

_____
_____
_____ Zip_____
Phone: Home _____ Work _____
_____

_____
_____ Zip_____
Phone: Home _____ Work _____
_____

_____
_____ Zip_____
Phone: Home _____ Work _____
_____

_____
_____ Zip_____
Phone: Home _____ Work _____
_____

_____
_____ Zip_____
Phone: Home _____ Work _____
_____

_____
_____ Zip_____
Phone: Home _____ Work _____
_____

_____
_____ Zip_____
Phone: Home _____ Work _____

name • address • phone

B

_____
_____
_____ Zip_____
Phone: Home _____ Work _____
_____

_____
_____
_____ Zip_____
Phone: Home _____ Work _____
_____

_____
_____
_____ Zip_____
Phone: Home _____ Work _____
_____

_____
_____
_____ Zip_____
Phone: Home _____ Work _____
_____

_____
_____
_____ Zip_____
Phone: Home _____ Work _____
_____

_____
_____
_____ Zip_____
Phone: Home _____ Work _____
_____

_____
_____
_____ Zip_____
Phone: Home _____ Work _____

B

name • address • phone

_____

_____

_____ Zip_____

Phone: Home _____ Work_____

_____

_____

_____ Zip_____

Phone: Home _____ Work_____

_____

_____

_____ Zip_____

Phone: Home _____ Work_____

_____

_____

_____ Zip_____

Phone: Home _____ Work_____

_____

_____

_____ Zip_____

Phone: Home _____ Work_____

_____

_____

_____ Zip_____

Phone: Home _____ Work_____

_____

_____

_____ Zip_____

Phone: Home _____ Work_____

name • address • phone

B

_____
_____
_____ Zip_____
Phone: Home _____ Work _____

_____
_____
_____ Zip_____
Phone: Home _____ Work _____

_____
_____
_____ Zip_____
Phone: Home _____ Work _____

_____
_____
_____ Zip_____
Phone: Home _____ Work _____

_____
_____
_____ Zip_____
Phone: Home _____ Work _____

_____
_____
_____ Zip_____
Phone: Home _____ Work _____

_____
_____
_____ Zip_____
Phone: Home _____ Work _____

C IS FOR CONDOMINIUMS, ALSO KNOWN AS "STOWE TRAILERS."

name • address • phone

C

_____
_____
_____ Zip_____
Phone: Home _____ Work _____
_____

_____
_____
_____ Zip_____
Phone: Home _____ Work _____
_____

_____
_____
_____ Zip_____
Phone: Home _____ Work _____
_____

_____
_____
_____ Zip_____
Phone: Home _____ Work _____
_____

_____
_____
_____ Zip_____
Phone: Home _____ Work _____
_____

_____
_____
_____ Zip_____
Phone: Home _____ Work _____
_____

_____
_____
_____ Zip_____
Phone: Home _____ Work _____

C

name • address • phone

_____
_____
_____ Zip_____
Phone: Home _____ Work_____
_____

_____
_____ Zip_____
Phone: Home _____ Work_____
_____

_____
_____ Zip_____
Phone: Home _____ Work_____
_____

_____
_____ Zip_____
Phone: Home _____ Work_____
_____

_____
_____ Zip_____
Phone: Home _____ Work_____
_____

_____
_____ Zip_____
Phone: Home _____ Work_____
_____

_____
_____ Zip_____
Phone: Home _____ Work_____

name • address • phone

C

_____

_____

_____ Zip_____

Phone: Home _____ Work _____

_____

_____

_____ Zip_____

Phone: Home _____ Work _____

_____

_____

_____ Zip_____

Phone: Home _____ Work _____

_____

_____

_____ Zip_____

Phone: Home _____ Work _____

_____

_____

_____ Zip_____

Phone: Home _____ Work _____

_____

_____

_____ Zip_____

Phone: Home _____ Work _____

_____

_____

_____ Zip_____

Phone: Home _____ Work _____

C

name • address • phone

_____

_____

_____ Zip_____

Phone: Home _____ Work _____

_____

_____

_____ Zip_____

Phone: Home _____ Work _____

_____

_____

_____ Zip_____

Phone: Home _____ Work _____

_____

_____

_____ Zip_____

Phone: Home _____ Work _____

_____

_____

_____ Zip_____

Phone: Home _____ Work _____

_____

_____

_____ Zip_____

Phone: Home _____ Work _____

_____

_____

_____ Zip_____

Phone: Home _____ Work _____

name • address • phone $\quad$ C

_____
_____
_____ Zip_____
Phone: Home _____ Work _____

_____
_____
_____ Zip_____
Phone: Home _____ Work _____

_____
_____
_____ Zip_____
Phone: Home _____ Work _____

_____
_____
_____ Zip_____
Phone: Home _____ Work _____

_____
_____
_____ Zip_____
Phone: Home _____ Work _____

_____
_____
_____ Zip_____
Phone: Home _____ Work _____

_____
_____
_____ Zip_____
Phone: Home _____ Work _____

D is for Deer season.

Things a Real Vermonter DOESN'T DO during deer season:

- Walk a Great Dane.
- Stand under an apple tree.
- Whip out a white handkerchief to blow his nose.[1]
- Step into an open field at dawn.[2]
- Carry a buck out of the woods.
- Move suddenly.
- Ask: "What's that long flashlight for?"
- Step into an open field at dusk.
- Cough.[3]
- Climb a tree in a black leather jacket.
- Hitchhike beside a "Deer Crossing" sign.[4]
- Step into an open field at any time.
- Take his wife to "camp."[5]
- Shoot a doe.[6]
- Work.

[1] It looks like a deer's tail (known to Real Vermonters as a "flag") flashing through the woods. Flags are favorite Flatlander targets.

[2] Unless accompanied by a brass band playing "Dixie."

[3] It sounds like a buck snorting.

[4] He gets behind a tree that will stop a 30-06 slug and STAYS there.

[5] The Real Vermonter knows the safest place to be during deer season is in deer camp. Thus, for those who go, we append several social conventions: Never leave a loaded rifle near the poker table; don't start talking about deer camp before Labor Day; never wait until opening day to go to "camp"; never serve pork and beans; never shave until after getting a buck.

[6] Shooting a doe is like a Flatlander skipping a wicket in croquet.

name • address • phone
D

_____
_____
_____ Zip_____
Phone: Home _____ Work _____
_____
_____
_____ Zip_____
Phone: Home _____ Work _____
_____
_____
_____ Zip_____
Phone: Home _____ Work _____
_____
_____
_____ Zip_____
Phone: Home _____ Work _____
_____
_____
_____ Zip_____
Phone: Home _____ Work _____
_____
_____
_____ Zip_____
Phone: Home _____ Work _____
_____
_____
_____ Zip_____
Phone: Home _____ Work _____

D   name • address • phone

_____

_____
_____ Zip_____
Phone: Home _____ Work _____

_____

_____ Zip_____
Phone: Home _____ Work _____

_____

_____ Zip_____
Phone: Home _____ Work _____

_____

_____ Zip_____
Phone: Home _____ Work _____

_____

_____ Zip_____
Phone: Home _____ Work _____

_____

_____ Zip_____
Phone: Home _____ Work _____

_____

_____ Zip_____
Phone: Home _____ Work _____

name • address • phone   D

_____

_____

_____ Zip _____
Phone: Home _____ Work _____

_____

_____

_____ Zip _____
Phone: Home _____ Work _____

_____

_____

_____ Zip _____
Phone: Home _____ Work _____

_____

_____

_____ Zip _____
Phone: Home _____ Work _____

_____

_____

_____ Zip _____
Phone: Home _____ Work _____

_____

_____

_____ Zip _____
Phone: Home _____ Work _____

_____

_____

_____ Zip _____
Phone: Home _____ Work _____

E is for Existence.

Real Vermonters know that much of what exists is not apparent to the naked eye. Accordingly, they harken to proofs for certain phenomena that hover beyond the curtain of empirical certitude.

I. The Real Vermonter's proofs of the existence of God:[1]

   a) peepers
   b) dry gas
   c) newborn calves
   d) Bondo
   e) teat cups
   f) "Amazing Grace"[2]
   g) duct tape
   h) wild geese

II. The Real Vermonter's proofs of the existence of original sin:

   a) mastitis
   b) the glacier[3]
   c) witch grass
   d) Boston Red Sox[4]
   e) coons in the corn[5]
   f) washboards
   g) Jane Fonda
   h) late frosts

III. Other phenomena and proofs:

   justice . . . . .a warm December
   democracy. . . . . . .Town Meeting
   stupidity . . . . .U. S. Court of Appeals[6]
   courage . . . . .going to the barn
   insanity . . . . .thermonuclear devices
   peace. . . . . .sleeping kittens

[1]Other than the ultimate proof: The WELCOME TO VERMONT sign on I-91 just north of the Massachusetts border.

[2]When sung by First Congregationalists.

[3]Which deposited 17,000,000,000 rocks in Vermont and lots of stones, too (most of which have turned up in Real Vermonters' gardens).

[4]East of the Mountains. West of the Mountains it's the New York Football Giants.

[5]Or in the garbage or in the chicken coop.

[6]For not allowing Vermont women to knit for profit in their homes.

name • address • phone   E

_____

_____
_____ Zip _____
Phone: Home _____ Work _____
_____

_____
_____ Zip _____
Phone: Home _____ Work _____
_____

_____
_____ Zip _____
Phone: Home _____ Work _____
_____

_____
_____ Zip _____
Phone: Home _____ Work _____
_____

_____
_____ Zip _____
Phone: Home _____ Work _____
_____

_____
_____ Zip _____
Phone: Home _____ Work _____
_____

_____ Zip _____
Phone: Home _____ Work _____

E

name • address • phone

_____
_____
_____ Zip _____
Phone: Home _____ Work _____
_____

_____
_____ Zip _____
Phone: Home _____ Work _____
_____

_____
_____ Zip _____
Phone: Home _____ Work _____
_____

_____
_____ Zip _____
Phone: Home _____ Work _____
_____

_____
_____ Zip _____
Phone: Home _____ Work _____
_____

_____
_____ Zip _____
Phone: Home _____ Work _____
_____

_____
_____ Zip _____
Phone: Home _____ Work _____

name • address • phone

E

_____

_____

_____ Zip _____

Phone: Home _____ Work _____

_____

_____

_____ Zip _____

Phone: Home _____ Work _____

_____

_____

_____ Zip _____

Phone: Home _____ Work _____

_____

_____

_____ Zip _____

Phone: Home _____ Work _____

_____

_____

_____ Zip _____

Phone: Home _____ Work _____

_____

_____

_____ Zip _____

Phone: Home _____ Work _____

_____

_____

_____ Zip _____

Phone: Home _____ Work _____

F is for Flatlanders.

Flatlanders are where you find them. Over the years Flatlanders have perfected the art of looking like Real Vermonters. There are a few places, however, where these creatures are still to be found in their natural habitats, doing what comes naturally. For some excellent Flatlander viewing, we suggest the following places:

- Top Notch (Stowe)
- Flynn Theater (Burlington)
- at roadside mailboxes[1]
- at a film[2]
- at a drive-in bank or ATM
- Basin Harbor Club (Vergennes)
- Common Ground Restaurant (Brattleboro)
- Weston Playhouse
- Marlboro Festival
- Goddard College (Plainfield)
- Orvis Fly Fishing School (Manchester)
- Killington, Okemo, Stowe, Jay, Stratton, and Sugarbush
- Weston Priory
- Olympiad (South Burlington)
- Bennington College
- Breadloaf Writers Conference (Ripton)
- The Cheese Outlet (Burlington)
- Weston Country Store
- Bread and Puppet Theater (Glover)
- The Woodstock Inn

[1] Waiting for trust fund checks.
[2] Real Vermonters go to the movies.

name • address • phone

F

_____

_____

_____ Zip_____
Phone: Home _____ Work _____

_____

_____

_____ Zip_____
Phone: Home _____ Work _____

_____

_____

_____ Zip_____
Phone: Home _____ Work _____

_____

_____

_____ Zip_____
Phone: Home _____ Work _____

_____

_____

_____ Zip_____
Phone: Home _____ Work _____

_____

_____

_____ Zip_____
Phone: Home _____ Work _____

_____

_____

_____ Zip_____
Phone: Home _____ Work _____

F

name • address • phone

_____

_____ Zip_____

Phone: Home _____ Work _____

_____

_____

_____ Zip_____

Phone: Home _____ Work _____

_____

_____

_____ Zip_____

Phone: Home _____ Work _____

_____

_____

_____ Zip_____

Phone: Home _____ Work _____

_____

_____

_____ Zip_____

Phone: Home _____ Work _____

_____

_____

_____ Zip_____

Phone: Home _____ Work _____

_____

_____

_____ Zip_____

Phone: Home _____ Work _____

name • address • phone   F

_____
_____
_____ Zip_____
Phone: Home _____ Work _____
_____
_____
_____ Zip_____
Phone: Home _____ Work _____
_____
_____
_____ Zip_____
Phone: Home _____ Work _____
_____
_____
_____ Zip_____
Phone: Home _____ Work _____
_____
_____
_____ Zip_____
Phone: Home _____ Work _____
_____
_____
_____ Zip_____
Phone: Home _____ Work _____
_____
_____
_____ Zip_____
Phone: Home _____ Work _____

G IS FOR GENIUS.

name • address • phone

G

_____
_____
_____ Zip_____
Phone: Home _____ Work _____

_____
_____
_____ Zip_____
Phone: Home _____ Work _____

_____
_____
_____ Zip_____
Phone: Home _____ Work _____

_____
_____
_____ Zip_____
Phone: Home _____ Work _____

_____
_____
_____ Zip_____
Phone: Home _____ Work _____

_____
_____
_____ Zip_____
Phone: Home _____ Work _____

_____
_____
_____ Zip_____
Phone: Home _____ Work _____

G   name • address • phone

_____

_____
_____ Zip _____
Phone: Home _____ Work _____

_____

_____
_____ Zip _____
Phone: Home _____ Work _____

_____

_____
_____ Zip _____
Phone: Home _____ Work _____

_____

_____
_____ Zip _____
Phone: Home _____ Work _____

_____

_____
_____ Zip _____
Phone: Home _____ Work _____

_____

_____
_____ Zip _____
Phone: Home _____ Work _____

_____

_____
_____ Zip _____
Phone: Home _____ Work _____

name • address • phone   G

_____

_____

_____ Zip _____
Phone: Home _____ Work _____

_____

_____ Zip _____
Phone: Home _____ Work _____

_____

_____ Zip _____
Phone: Home _____ Work _____

_____

_____ Zip _____
Phone: Home _____ Work _____

_____

_____ Zip _____
Phone: Home _____ Work _____

_____

_____ Zip _____
Phone: Home _____ Work _____

_____

_____ Zip _____
Phone: Home _____ Work _____

H is for History.

Here's the Real Vermonter's view of World History.

Bad Happenings		Good Happenings
	The Beginning of Time	
		Nothing of significance occurs
	1609	Discovery of Lake Champlain
	1739	Birth of Ethan Allen
New Hampshire Grants declared part of New York	1764	
	1775	Ethan Allen captures Fort Ticonderoga
Vermont named "New Connecticut" Fort Ticonderoga falls to the British	1777	The Republic of Vermont is born
	1791	
	Vermont enters the Union[1]	
The year of "no summer"[2]	1816	
	1860	Lincoln is elected
	1863	The Emancipation Proclamation
The Great Flood	1927	
Democrats make a great breakthrough	1952	
I-91 completed	1978	
	1982	178 Vermont Town Meetings vote for a nuclear weapons freeze

[1] The debate over whether this was a "good" or "bad" happening still rages within the ranks of Real Vermonters.

[2] Real Vermonters like to tell the story of "eighteen hundred and froze-to-death" to Flatlanders. It snowed every month that year. Right after an April snowfall is the best time to tell the story.

name • address • phone

H

_____
_____
_____ Zip_____
Phone: Home _____ Work _____

_____
_____
_____ Zip_____
Phone: Home _____ Work _____

_____
_____
_____ Zip_____
Phone: Home _____ Work _____

_____
_____
_____ Zip_____
Phone: Home _____ Work _____

_____
_____
_____ Zip_____
Phone: Home _____ Work _____

_____
_____
_____ Zip_____
Phone: Home _____ Work _____

_____
_____
_____ Zip_____
Phone: Home _____ Work _____

H

name • address • phone

_____

_____

_____ Zip_____

Phone: Home _____ Work _____

_____

_____

_____ Zip_____

Phone: Home _____ Work _____

_____

_____

_____ Zip_____

Phone: Home _____ Work _____

_____

_____

_____ Zip_____

Phone: Home _____ Work _____

_____

_____

_____ Zip_____

Phone: Home _____ Work _____

_____

_____

_____ Zip_____

Phone: Home _____ Work _____

_____

_____

_____ Zip_____

Phone: Home _____ Work _____

name • address • phone   H

_____

_____

_____ Zip _____

Phone: Home _____ Work _____

_____

_____ Zip _____

Phone: Home _____ Work _____

_____

_____ Zip _____

Phone: Home _____ Work _____

_____

_____ Zip _____

Phone: Home _____ Work _____

_____

_____ Zip _____

Phone: Home _____ Work _____

_____

_____ Zip _____

Phone: Home _____ Work _____

_____

_____ Zip _____

Phone: Home _____ Work _____

H name • address • phone

_____
_____
_____ Zip_____
Phone: Home _____ Work_____
_____

_____
_____ Zip_____
Phone: Home _____ Work_____
_____

_____
_____ Zip_____
Phone: Home _____ Work_____
_____

_____
_____ Zip_____
Phone: Home _____ Work_____
_____

_____
_____ Zip_____
Phone: Home _____ Work_____
_____

_____
_____ Zip_____
Phone: Home _____ Work_____
_____

_____
_____ Zip_____
Phone: Home _____ Work_____

name • address • phone   H

_____

_____ Zip_____

Phone: Home _____ Work _____

_____

_____ Zip_____

Phone: Home _____ Work _____

_____

_____ Zip_____

Phone: Home _____ Work _____

_____

_____ Zip_____

Phone: Home _____ Work _____

_____

_____ Zip_____

Phone: Home _____ Work _____

_____

_____ Zip_____

Phone: Home _____ Work _____

_____

_____ Zip_____

Phone: Home _____ Work _____

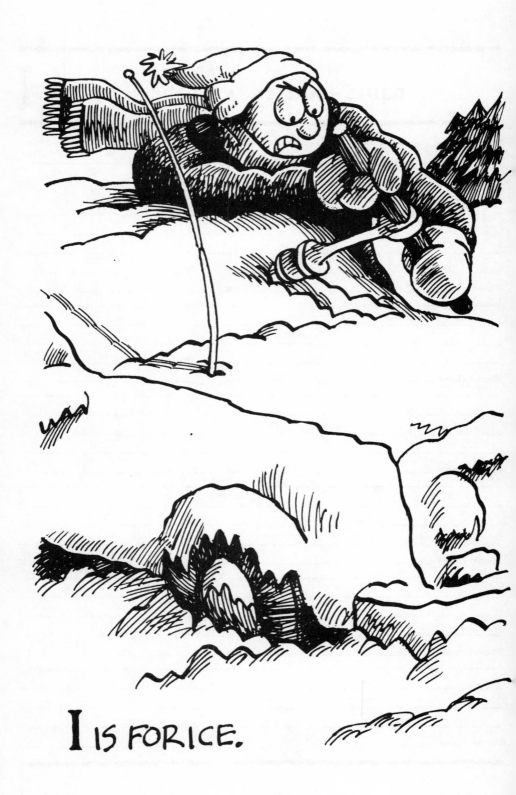

I IS FOR ICE.

name • address • phone

I

_____
_____
_____ Zip _____
Phone: Home _____ Work _____

_____
_____
_____ Zip _____
Phone: Home _____ Work _____

_____
_____
_____ Zip _____
Phone: Home _____ Work _____

_____
_____
_____ Zip _____
Phone: Home _____ Work _____

_____
_____
_____ Zip _____
Phone: Home _____ Work _____

_____
_____
_____ Zip _____
Phone: Home _____ Work _____

_____
_____
_____ Zip _____
Phone: Home _____ Work _____

I

name • address • phone

_____

_____

_____ Zip _____
Phone: Home _____ Work _____

_____

_____

_____ Zip _____
Phone: Home _____ Work _____

_____

_____

_____ Zip _____
Phone: Home _____ Work _____

_____

_____

_____ Zip _____
Phone: Home _____ Work _____

_____

_____

_____ Zip _____
Phone: Home _____ Work _____

_____

_____

_____ Zip _____
Phone: Home _____ Work _____

_____

_____

_____ Zip _____
Phone: Home _____ Work _____

name • address • phone

I

_____
_____
_____ Zip_____
Phone: Home _____ Work _____

_____
_____
_____ Zip_____
Phone: Home _____ Work _____

_____
_____
_____ Zip_____
Phone: Home _____ Work _____

_____
_____
_____ Zip_____
Phone: Home _____ Work _____

_____
_____
_____ Zip_____
Phone: Home _____ Work _____

_____
_____
_____ Zip_____
Phone: Home _____ Work _____

_____
_____
_____ Zip_____
Phone: Home _____ Work _____

J is for Jokes.

Bryan and Mares Three Favorite Vermont Jokes

A Flatlander stopped to ask a Real Vermonter directions. "How do you get to Rutland?"

"Don't know," said the Real Vermonter.

"Well, then, can you tell me how to get to Route 7?"

"Can't say as I can."

"Well," said the now exasperated Flatlander, "do you know where the Mendon road is?"

"Nope."

"You don't know much, do you?" growled the Flatlander.

"Ain't lost."

□ □ □ □ □

The Flatlander parked his car on the side of a very muddy road in the Northeast Kingdom. Looking across the road to where he wanted to be, he saw a Real Vermonter sitting on his front porch. "How'd you get over there?" the Flatlander cried.

"Born here."

□ □ □ □ □

A Flatlander driving on a Vermont backroad came upon a farmer struggling to remove large rocks from his field. He stopped, got out, and asked: "What you doing?"

Through locked jaws the farmer grunted, "Pickin' stone."

"Where'd the stones come from?"

"Glacier brought 'em," he replied without looking up.

"Where'd the glacier go?" asked the Flatlander.

"Back to get more stone!"

name • address • phone

J

_____

_____

_____ Zip_____

Phone: Home _____ Work _____

_____

_____

_____ Zip_____

Phone: Home _____ Work _____

_____

_____

_____ Zip_____

Phone: Home _____ Work _____

_____

_____

_____ Zip_____

Phone: Home _____ Work _____

_____

_____

_____ Zip_____

Phone: Home _____ Work _____

_____

_____

_____ Zip_____

Phone: Home _____ Work _____

_____

_____

_____ Zip_____

Phone: Home _____ Work _____

J

name • address • phone

_____

_____

_____ Zip_____

Phone: Home _____ Work _____

_____

_____

_____ Zip_____

Phone: Home _____ Work _____

_____

_____

_____ Zip_____

Phone: Home _____ Work _____

_____

_____

_____ Zip_____

Phone: Home _____ Work _____

_____

_____

_____ Zip_____

Phone: Home _____ Work _____

_____

_____

_____ Zip_____

Phone: Home _____ Work _____

_____

_____

_____ Zip_____

Phone: Home _____ Work _____

name • address • phone

J

_____

_____

_____ Zip_____

Phone: Home _____ Work _____

_____

_____

_____ Zip_____

Phone: Home _____ Work _____

_____

_____

_____ Zip_____

Phone: Home _____ Work _____

_____

_____

_____ Zip_____

Phone: Home _____ Work _____

_____

_____

_____ Zip_____

Phone: Home _____ Work _____

_____

_____

_____ Zip_____

Phone: Home _____ Work _____

_____

_____

_____ Zip_____

Phone: Home _____ Work _____

K IS FOR KITCHEN, A REAL VERMONTER'S PARLOR.

name • address • phone K

_____
_____
_____
_____ Zip_____
Phone: Home _____ Work _____
_____
_____
_____
_____ Zip_____
Phone: Home _____ Work _____
_____
_____
_____
_____ Zip_____
Phone: Home _____ Work _____
_____
_____
_____
_____ Zip_____
Phone: Home _____ Work _____
_____
_____
_____
_____ Zip_____
Phone: Home _____ Work _____
_____
_____
_____
_____ Zip_____
Phone: Home _____ Work _____
_____
_____
_____
_____ Zip_____
Phone: Home _____ Work _____

K name • address • phone

_____
_____
_____
_____ Zip_____
Phone: Home _____ Work _____

_____
_____
_____ Zip_____
Phone: Home _____ Work _____

_____
_____
_____ Zip_____
Phone: Home _____ Work _____

_____
_____
_____ Zip_____
Phone: Home _____ Work _____

_____
_____
_____ Zip_____
Phone: Home _____ Work _____

_____
_____
_____ Zip_____
Phone: Home _____ Work _____

_____
_____
_____ Zip_____
Phone: Home _____ Work _____

name • address • phone

K

_____
_____
_____ Zip_____
Phone: Home _____ Work _____
_____

_____
_____
_____ Zip_____
Phone: Home _____ Work _____
_____

_____
_____
_____ Zip_____
Phone: Home _____ Work _____
_____

_____
_____
_____ Zip_____
Phone: Home _____ Work _____
_____

_____
_____
_____ Zip_____
Phone: Home _____ Work _____
_____

_____
_____
_____ Zip_____
Phone: Home _____ Work _____
_____

_____
_____
_____ Zip_____
Phone: Home _____ Work _____

L is for Lists.

Real Vermonters are fond of keeping lists. We've started three lists but left room for you to add to them.

Things Real Vermonters have to explain to Flatlanders:

1. Why farmers spread all that manure on fresh white snow.
2. Why not to yell "Go, go!" at an ox pull.[1]
3. _____
4. _____

Things Flatlanders have to explain to Real Vermonters:

1. Why it's a drag to have a Real Vermonter's cow in their garden.[2]
2. Venture capital.
3. _____
4. _____

Things neither can explain:[3]

1. Why dog "doo" smells worse than cow "doo."
2. The United Nations.
3. _____
4. _____

---

[1] It sounds like "Whoa, whoa!" and often stops the team dead in its tracks.

[2] Often followed by an explanation of the difference between a compost heap and a manure pile.

[3] There is, of course, a list of things that even Real Vermonters have trouble explaining to each other. For example, why some of them use Harvestore silos, why it is important to vote Democrat (once in a while), and how to get from Goshen to Avery's Gore in February.

name • address • phone

L

_____
_____
_____
_____ Zip _____
Phone: Home _____ Work _____

_____
_____
_____ Zip _____
Phone: Home _____ Work _____

_____
_____
_____ Zip _____
Phone: Home _____ Work _____

_____
_____
_____ Zip _____
Phone: Home _____ Work _____

_____
_____
_____ Zip _____
Phone: Home _____ Work _____

_____
_____
_____ Zip _____
Phone: Home _____ Work _____

_____
_____
_____ Zip _____
Phone: Home _____ Work _____

L

name • address • phone

_____
_____
_____ Zip _____
Phone: Home _____ Work _____
_____
_____
_____ Zip _____
Phone: Home _____ Work _____
_____
_____
_____ Zip _____
Phone: Home _____ Work _____
_____
_____
_____ Zip _____
Phone: Home _____ Work _____
_____
_____
_____ Zip _____
Phone: Home _____ Work _____
_____
_____
_____ Zip _____
Phone: Home _____ Work _____
_____
_____
_____ Zip _____
Phone: Home _____ Work _____

name • address • phone

L

_____
_____
_____
_____ Zip_____
Phone: Home _____ Work _____
_____

_____
_____
_____ Zip_____
Phone: Home _____ Work _____
_____

_____
_____
_____ Zip_____
Phone: Home _____ Work _____
_____

_____
_____
_____ Zip_____
Phone: Home _____ Work _____
_____

_____
_____
_____ Zip_____
Phone: Home _____ Work _____
_____

_____
_____
_____ Zip_____
Phone: Home _____ Work _____
_____

_____
_____
_____ Zip_____
Phone: Home _____ Work _____

L

name • address • phone

_____
_____
_____ Zip_____
Phone: Home _____ Work _____
_____
_____
_____
_____ Zip_____
Phone: Home _____ Work _____
_____
_____
_____
_____ Zip_____
Phone: Home _____ Work _____
_____
_____
_____
_____ Zip_____
Phone: Home _____ Work _____
_____
_____
_____
_____ Zip_____
Phone: Home _____ Work _____
_____
_____
_____
_____ Zip_____
Phone: Home _____ Work _____
_____
_____
_____
_____ Zip_____
Phone: Home _____ Work _____

name • address • phone   L

_____
_____
_____ Zip_____
Phone: Home _____ Work _____

_____
_____
_____ Zip_____
Phone: Home _____ Work _____

_____
_____
_____ Zip_____
Phone: Home _____ Work _____

_____
_____
_____ Zip_____
Phone: Home _____ Work _____

_____
_____
_____ Zip_____
Phone: Home _____ Work _____

_____
_____
_____ Zip_____
Phone: Home _____ Work _____

_____
_____
_____ Zip_____
Phone: Home _____ Work _____

M IS FOR MOOSE.

name • address • phone M

_____

_____

_____ Zip_____
Phone: Home _____ Work _____

_____

_____

_____ Zip_____
Phone: Home _____ Work _____

_____

_____

_____ Zip_____
Phone: Home _____ Work _____

_____

_____

_____ Zip_____
Phone: Home _____ Work _____

_____

_____

_____ Zip_____
Phone: Home _____ Work _____

_____

_____

_____ Zip_____
Phone: Home _____ Work _____

_____

_____

_____ Zip_____
Phone: Home _____ Work _____

M name • address • phone

_____
_____
_____ Zip _____
Phone: Home _____ Work _____
_____

_____
_____
_____ Zip _____
Phone: Home _____ Work _____
_____

_____
_____
_____ Zip _____
Phone: Home _____ Work _____
_____

_____
_____
_____ Zip _____
Phone: Home _____ Work _____
_____

_____
_____
_____ Zip _____
Phone: Home _____ Work _____
_____

_____
_____
_____ Zip _____
Phone: Home _____ Work _____
_____

_____
_____
_____ Zip _____
Phone: Home _____ Work _____

name • address • phone   M

_____
_____
_____ Zip_____
Phone: Home _____ Work _____

_____
_____
_____ Zip_____
Phone: Home _____ Work _____

_____
_____
_____ Zip_____
Phone: Home _____ Work _____

_____
_____
_____ Zip_____
Phone: Home _____ Work _____

_____
_____
_____ Zip_____
Phone: Home _____ Work _____

_____
_____
_____ Zip_____
Phone: Home _____ Work _____

_____
_____
_____ Zip_____
Phone: Home _____ Work _____

M name • address • phone

_____
_____
_____
_____ Zip_____
Phone: Home _____ Work _____

_____
_____
_____ Zip_____
Phone: Home _____ Work _____

_____
_____
_____ Zip_____
Phone: Home _____ Work _____

_____
_____
_____ Zip_____
Phone: Home _____ Work _____

_____
_____
_____ Zip_____
Phone: Home _____ Work _____

_____
_____
_____ Zip_____
Phone: Home _____ Work _____

_____
_____ Zip_____
Phone: Home _____ Work _____

name • address • phone

M

_____

_____

_____ Zip_____

Phone: Home _____ Work _____

_____

_____

_____ Zip_____

Phone: Home _____ Work _____

_____

_____

_____ Zip_____

Phone: Home _____ Work _____

_____

_____

_____ Zip_____

Phone: Home _____ Work _____

_____

_____

_____ Zip_____

Phone: Home _____ Work _____

_____

_____

_____ Zip_____

Phone: Home _____ Work _____

_____

_____

_____ Zip_____

Phone: Home _____ Work _____

N is for New Hampshire.

Vermonters have always had a "lover's quarrel" with the Granite State.[1] We have never forgiven her for John Stark,[2] or for having mountains higher than ours. We envy her seaport, but will never admit it. Vermonters will say that the best thing about New Hampshire is that the view of Vermont is better from there. They acknowledge, however, that Vermont's best known postcard (after the one of East Corinth village) shows the Placey farm in Newbury, featuring New Hampshire's river (the Connecticut) and New Hampshire's mountains (the White).

The Real Vermonter's favorite contemporary New Hampshire writer is Donald Hall, who lives in Danbury. In the January issue of *Esquire,*[3] he wrote: "Heaven knows, Vermont is a beautiful state, with pockets of real country remaining, but it is the *chic* northern New England rural retreat, not New Hampshire. . . . To Vermont go summering professors of philosophy, Dada poets from New Jersey, and CEOs. The result is Woodstock, where orthopedic surgeons wear checked shirts from L. L. Bean and play at being country folk, in the spirit of Marie Antoinette dressing up as a milkmaid."

The Real Vermonter's favorite explanation of the difference between the two states comes again from Frost: "Anything that can be said of Vermont can be said of New Hampshire as well, except in their mountains. Vermont's stretch straight and true, while New Hampshire's curl up in a coil."

---

[1]We borrow lovingly from Robert Frost who "quarreled" with the world and who observed that "New Hampshire is one of the best states in the Union. Vermont's the other." One of the Real Vermonter's best kept secrets is that Frost farmed on the flanks of New Hampshire's White Mountains and came to us by way of England, Massachusetts, and birth in (of all places) California.

[2]He was a New Hampshire general who won Vermont's most famous battle, The Battle of Bennington, in 1777. The battle was fought in New York, but we got the monument.

[3]A magazine which, of course, no Real Vermonter would ever read.

name • address • phone   N

_____
_____
_____ Zip_____
Phone: Home _____ Work _____

_____
_____
_____ Zip_____
Phone: Home _____ Work _____

_____
_____
_____ Zip_____
Phone: Home _____ Work _____

_____
_____
_____ Zip_____
Phone: Home _____ Work _____

_____
_____
_____ Zip_____
Phone: Home _____ Work _____

_____
_____
_____ Zip_____
Phone: Home _____ Work _____

_____
_____
_____ Zip_____
Phone: Home _____ Work _____

N

name • address • phone

_____

_____

_____ Zip _____
Phone: Home _____ Work _____

_____

_____ Zip _____
Phone: Home _____ Work _____

_____

_____ Zip _____
Phone: Home _____ Work _____

_____

_____ Zip _____
Phone: Home _____ Work _____

_____

_____ Zip _____
Phone: Home _____ Work _____

_____

_____ Zip _____
Phone: Home _____ Work _____

_____

_____ Zip _____
Phone: Home _____ Work _____

name • address • phone N

_____

_____

_____ Zip_____

Phone: Home _____ Work _____

_____

_____

_____ Zip_____

Phone: Home _____ Work _____

_____

_____

_____ Zip_____

Phone: Home _____ Work _____

_____

_____

_____ Zip_____

Phone: Home _____ Work _____

_____

_____

_____ Zip_____

Phone: Home _____ Work _____

_____

_____

_____ Zip_____

Phone: Home _____ Work _____

_____

_____

_____ Zip_____

Phone: Home _____ Work _____

O is for Omissions.

The modern world is full of ideas, gadgets, and other devices deemed vital by manufacturers, advertisers, and other flatlanders. Real Vermonters, however, simply don't see the need for many of these items.

Real Vermonters don't have in their homes:

1. Cordless phones
2. Portraits of their dogs
3. *The Woodcutter's Companion*
4. A doorbell that plays "America the Beautiful"
5. Wind chimes
6. "Family rooms"[1]

Real Vermonters don't have on their persons:

1. Passports
2. Appointment books
3. Compasses
4. Swiss Army knives
5. Money clips
6. Cross pens

Real Vermonters don't have in their yards:

1. Stacks of designer firewood[2]
2. Barbecue pits
3. Neighbors with cocktails in their hands
4. Swing sets from Childcraft
5. "Keep off the grass" signs
6. Sailboats or windsurfers[3]

[1] Real Vermont families use the entire house.
[2] Perfectly shaped, plastic-wrapped bundles of firewood. Sold in Flatlanders General Stores at $1,765.00 a cord.
[3] And especially not "ultralights."

name • address • phone

_____
_____
_____ Zip _____
Phone: Home _____ Work _____
_____
_____
_____ Zip _____
Phone: Home _____ Work _____
_____
_____
_____ Zip _____
Phone: Home _____ Work _____
_____
_____
_____ Zip _____
Phone: Home _____ Work _____
_____
_____
_____ Zip _____
Phone: Home _____ Work _____
_____
_____
_____ Zip _____
Phone: Home _____ Work _____
_____
_____
_____ Zip _____
Phone: Home _____ Work _____

O

name • address • phone

_____
_____
_____ Zip_____
Phone: Home _____ Work_____
_____

_____
_____ Zip_____
Phone: Home _____ Work_____
_____

_____
_____ Zip_____
Phone: Home _____ Work_____
_____

_____
_____ Zip_____
Phone: Home _____ Work_____
_____

_____
_____ Zip_____
Phone: Home _____ Work_____
_____

_____
_____ Zip_____
Phone: Home _____ Work_____
_____

_____
_____ Zip_____
Phone: Home _____ Work_____

name • address • phone

O

_____

_____
_____ Zip_____
Phone: Home _____ Work _____

_____

_____
_____ Zip_____
Phone: Home _____ Work _____

_____

_____
_____ Zip_____
Phone: Home _____ Work _____

_____

_____
_____ Zip_____
Phone: Home _____ Work _____

_____

_____
_____ Zip_____
Phone: Home _____ Work _____

_____

_____
_____ Zip_____
Phone: Home _____ Work _____

_____

_____
_____ Zip_____
Phone: Home _____ Work _____

P is for Politics.

In politics as in cows and seasons Real Vermonters have their favorites. Here are some:

FAVORITE TELEVISED POLITICAL AD

Deane Davis and His Rowboat

(Because it tempted Hilton Wick to produce the Bumper Car ad of 1984 and thereby provide comic relief for what was otherwise a very dull political season.[1])

FAVORITE DIPLOMATIC GAFFE

Warren Austin in the United Nations in 1949

(Austin, a Real Vermonter and America's first Ambassador to the UN, rose in exasperation during a bitter debate between Middle Eastern nations and suggested that the Arabs and Jews get together and "settle this problem in a true Christian spirit!"[2])

FAVORITE ROLL CALL VOTE

The Vote on the Hunter Orange Bill in 1974

(Because it identified every Flatlander in the Vermont House of Representatives—at least for that year.[3])

[1] In 1968 Governor Davis humanized himself by rolling up his pants and bailing our a rowboat on Lake Champlain. The ad received international acclaim for effectiveness. In 1984 Hilton Wick succeeded only in looking silly by squeezing into a kiddie bumper car at a carnival.

[2] Our thanks to Jim Pacy, a Hungarian New Jerseyite, who, with magnificence, teaches Real Vermonter's kids diplomacy at UVM.

[3] The bill specified that every deer hunter "shall wear an outer garment that is of hunter orange color, has a total surface of at least 100 square inches and is worn above the waist." Game wardens, man your measuring tapes! Politics does indeed make strange bed persons—Madeleine Kunin and Richard Snelling both voted "yes." So, to his perpetual embarrassment, did Bob Kinsey of Craftsbury.

name • address • phone

P

_____
_____
_____ Zip_____
Phone: Home _____ Work _____

_____
_____
_____ Zip_____
Phone: Home _____ Work _____

_____
_____
_____ Zip_____
Phone: Home _____ Work _____

_____
_____
_____ Zip_____
Phone: Home _____ Work _____

_____
_____
_____ Zip_____
Phone: Home _____ Work _____

_____
_____
_____ Zip_____
Phone: Home _____ Work _____

_____
_____
_____ Zip_____
Phone: Home _____ Work _____

P

name • address • phone

_____

_____

_____ Zip_____

Phone: Home _____ Work _____

_____

_____

_____ Zip_____

Phone: Home _____ Work _____

_____

_____

_____ Zip_____

Phone: Home _____ Work _____

_____

_____

_____ Zip_____

Phone: Home _____ Work _____

_____

_____

_____ Zip_____

Phone: Home _____ Work _____

_____

_____

_____ Zip_____

Phone: Home _____ Work _____

_____

_____

_____ Zip_____

Phone: Home _____ Work _____

name • address • phone

P

_____
_____
_____ Zip _____
Phone: Home _____ Work _____

_____
_____ Zip _____
Phone: Home _____ Work _____

_____
_____ Zip _____
Phone: Home _____ Work _____

_____
_____ Zip _____
Phone: Home _____ Work _____

_____
_____ Zip _____
Phone: Home _____ Work _____

_____
_____ Zip _____
Phone: Home _____ Work _____

_____
_____ Zip _____
Phone: Home _____ Work _____

P

name • address • phone

_____

_____

_____ Zip_____
Phone: Home _____ Work _____

_____

_____

_____ Zip_____
Phone: Home _____ Work _____

_____

_____

_____ Zip_____
Phone: Home _____ Work _____

_____

_____

_____ Zip_____
Phone: Home _____ Work _____

_____

_____

_____ Zip_____
Phone: Home _____ Work _____

_____

_____

_____ Zip_____
Phone: Home _____ Work _____

_____

_____

_____ Zip_____
Phone: Home _____ Work _____

name • address • phone   P

_____

_____
_____ Zip _____
Phone: Home _____ Work _____

_____

_____
_____ Zip _____
Phone: Home _____ Work _____

_____

_____
_____ Zip _____
Phone: Home _____ Work _____

_____

_____
_____ Zip _____
Phone: Home _____ Work _____

_____

_____
_____ Zip _____
Phone: Home _____ Work _____

_____

_____
_____ Zip _____
Phone: Home _____ Work _____

_____

_____
_____ Zip _____
Phone: Home _____ Work _____

Q is for Quixote.

Quixote is the Don of "the impossible dream." Vermont cousins include:

- Danny Gore and his quest for the Governor's chair.
- Herb Ogden and his efforts to change the property tax.
- Frank Bryan trying to save Town Meeting for use in the 21st century.
- Any farmer struggling to clear all the boulders from his fields.
- The people of Chittenden County trying to win favor in the eyes of the rest of the state.
- A Flatlander searching for a Cuisinart repairman in Canaan.
- Dick Snelling and his attempt to convince people that when 90 state troopers and 50 social workers arrive at dawn to take 112 children away from their parents for 72 hours of "examination," it is not a "raid."
- A hiker looking for 60 cubic feet of solitude on the top of Mt. Mansfield.
- Dairy farmers fighting imitation milk products.
- A car owner and his search for a salt-resistent undercoating.
- Anyone searching for an unbreakable axe handle.
- A driver leaving Lyndon Corner for Greensboro Bend during mud season.
- Ice fishermen getting their shanties off Bomoseen in April.
- President Lattie F. Coor and his annual pilgrimage to Montpelier to impress the legislature with "this year's fiscal crisis" at UVM.

name • address • phone

_____
_____
_____ Zip_____
Phone: Home _____ Work _____

_____
_____
_____ Zip_____
Phone: Home _____ Work _____

_____
_____
_____ Zip_____
Phone: Home _____ Work _____

_____
_____
_____ Zip_____
Phone: Home _____ Work _____

_____
_____
_____ Zip_____
Phone: Home _____ Work _____

_____
_____
_____ Zip_____
Phone: Home _____ Work _____

_____
_____
_____ Zip_____
Phone: Home _____ Work _____

R IS FOR "REAL" TRUCK.

name • address • phone

R

_____

_____

_____ Zip_____
Phone: Home _____ Work_____

_____

_____

_____ Zip_____
Phone: Home _____ Work_____

_____

_____

_____ Zip_____
Phone: Home _____ Work_____

_____

_____

_____ Zip_____
Phone: Home _____ Work_____

_____

_____

_____ Zip_____
Phone: Home _____ Work_____

_____

_____

_____ Zip_____
Phone: Home _____ Work_____

_____

_____

_____ Zip_____
Phone: Home _____ Work_____

R

name • address • phone

_____
_____
_____ Zip_____
Phone: Home _____ Work _____
_____

_____
_____
_____ Zip_____
Phone: Home _____ Work _____
_____

_____
_____
_____ Zip_____
Phone: Home _____ Work _____
_____

_____
_____
_____ Zip_____
Phone: Home _____ Work _____
_____

_____
_____
_____ Zip_____
Phone: Home _____ Work _____
_____

_____
_____
_____ Zip_____
Phone: Home _____ Work _____
_____

_____
_____
_____ Zip_____
Phone: Home _____ Work _____

name • address • phone

R

_____

_____

_____ Zip _____

Phone: Home _____ Work _____

_____

_____

_____ Zip _____

Phone: Home _____ Work _____

_____

_____

_____ Zip _____

Phone: Home _____ Work _____

_____

_____

_____ Zip _____

Phone: Home _____ Work _____

_____

_____

_____ Zip _____

Phone: Home _____ Work _____

_____

_____

_____ Zip _____

Phone: Home _____ Work _____

_____

_____

_____ Zip _____

Phone: Home _____ Work _____

R

name • address • phone

_____

_____

_____ Zip_____

Phone: Home _____ Work _____

_____

_____

_____ Zip_____

Phone: Home _____ Work _____

_____

_____

_____ Zip_____

Phone: Home _____ Work _____

_____

_____

_____ Zip_____

Phone: Home _____ Work _____

_____

_____

_____ Zip_____

Phone: Home _____ Work _____

_____

_____

_____ Zip_____

Phone: Home _____ Work _____

_____

_____

_____ Zip_____

Phone: Home _____ Work _____

name • address • phone

R

_____

_____ Zip _____
Phone: Home _____ Work _____
_____

_____

_____ Zip _____
Phone: Home _____ Work _____
_____

_____

_____ Zip _____
Phone: Home _____ Work _____
_____

_____

_____ Zip _____
Phone: Home _____ Work _____
_____

_____

_____ Zip _____
Phone: Home _____ Work _____
_____

_____

_____ Zip _____
Phone: Home _____ Work _____
_____

_____

_____ Zip _____
Phone: Home _____ Work _____

S IS FOR SUNBATHING.

name • address • phone

S

_____
_____
_____
_____ Zip_____
Phone: Home _____ Work _____
_____
_____
_____
_____ Zip_____
Phone: Home _____ Work _____
_____
_____
_____
_____ Zip_____
Phone: Home _____ Work _____
_____
_____
_____
_____ Zip_____
Phone: Home _____ Work _____
_____
_____
_____
_____ Zip_____
Phone: Home _____ Work _____
_____
_____
_____
_____ Zip_____
Phone: Home _____ Work _____
_____
_____
_____
_____ Zip_____
Phone: Home _____ Work _____

S

name • address • phone

_____

_____ Zip_____

Phone: Home _____ Work_____

_____

_____

_____ Zip_____

Phone: Home _____ Work_____

_____

_____

_____ Zip_____

Phone: Home _____ Work_____

_____

_____

_____ Zip_____

Phone: Home _____ Work_____

_____

_____

_____ Zip_____

Phone: Home _____ Work_____

_____

_____

_____ Zip_____

Phone: Home _____ Work_____

_____

_____

_____ Zip_____

Phone: Home _____ Work_____

name • address • phone S

_____
_____
_____ Zip_____
Phone: Home _____ Work _____

_____
_____
_____ Zip_____
Phone: Home _____ Work _____

_____
_____
_____ Zip_____
Phone: Home _____ Work _____

_____
_____
_____ Zip_____
Phone: Home _____ Work _____

_____
_____
_____ Zip_____
Phone: Home _____ Work _____

_____
_____
_____ Zip_____
Phone: Home _____ Work _____

_____
_____
_____ Zip_____
Phone: Home _____ Work _____

S

name • address • phone

_____

_____
_____ Zip_____
Phone: Home _____ Work_____

_____

_____
_____ Zip_____
Phone: Home _____ Work_____

_____

_____
_____ Zip_____
Phone: Home _____ Work_____

_____

_____
_____ Zip_____
Phone: Home _____ Work_____

_____

_____
_____ Zip_____
Phone: Home _____ Work_____

_____

_____
_____ Zip_____
Phone: Home _____ Work_____

_____

_____
_____ Zip_____
Phone: Home _____ Work_____

name • address • phone $\quad$ S

_____
_____
_____ Zip_____
Phone: Home _____ Work_____
_____

_____
_____
_____ Zip_____
Phone: Home _____ Work_____
_____

_____
_____
_____ Zip_____
Phone: Home _____ Work_____
_____

_____
_____
_____ Zip_____
Phone: Home _____ Work_____
_____

_____
_____
_____ Zip_____
Phone: Home _____ Work_____
_____

_____
_____
_____ Zip_____
Phone: Home _____ Work_____
_____

_____
_____
_____ Zip_____
Phone: Home _____ Work_____

T is for Things.

Things Real Vermonters don't worry about:

- the "greenhouse effect"[1]
- where to bury "Muffy" when she dies
- getting a package "there" overnight
- male menopause
- how to tie up their tomatoes
- snow
- a cold May[2]
- the "worst-possible-case scenario"
- parenting
- when to plant the peas
- cash-flow problems[3]
- who does Dan Rather's hair
- how to cross a barbed wire fence
- which way to turn the wheel when they go into a skid
- how to build a fire
- the difference between a weed and a vegetable
- when to cover the tomatoes
- whether or not the fence is "on"[4]
- cholesterol

[1] Many Real Vermonters actually look forward to the greenhouse effect and only hope it comes in their lifetime.

[2] According to Real Vermonters, "A cold May is kindly and fills the barn finely."

[3] Tom Slayton says, "Real Vermonters don't live so much on income as they do on lack of expense."

[4] Special Real Vermonter tips for telling when it's "on" if you are unsure: a) grab it, b) have your kid grab it, c) send a high-tailed dog under it. If a Real Vermonter tells you to urinate on it—DON'T.

name • address • phone

T

_____
_____
_____ Zip _____
Phone: Home _____ Work _____

_____
_____
_____ Zip _____
Phone: Home _____ Work _____

_____
_____
_____ Zip _____
Phone: Home _____ Work _____

_____
_____
_____ Zip _____
Phone: Home _____ Work _____

_____
_____
_____ Zip _____
Phone: Home _____ Work _____

_____
_____
_____ Zip _____
Phone: Home _____ Work _____

_____
_____
_____ Zip _____
Phone: Home _____ Work _____

T name • address • phone

_____
_____
_____ Zip_____
Phone: Home _____ Work _____

_____
_____
_____ Zip_____
Phone: Home _____ Work _____

_____
_____
_____ Zip_____
Phone: Home _____ Work _____

_____
_____
_____ Zip_____
Phone: Home _____ Work _____

_____
_____
_____ Zip_____
Phone: Home _____ Work _____

_____
_____
_____ Zip_____
Phone: Home _____ Work _____

_____
_____ Zip_____
Phone: Home _____ Work _____

name • address • phone   T

_____

_____

_____ Zip_____
Phone: Home _____ Work _____

_____

_____

_____ Zip_____
Phone: Home _____ Work _____

_____

_____

_____ Zip_____
Phone: Home _____ Work _____

_____

_____

_____ Zip_____
Phone: Home _____ Work _____

_____

_____

_____ Zip_____
Phone: Home _____ Work _____

_____

_____

_____ Zip_____
Phone: Home _____ Work _____

_____

_____

_____ Zip_____
Phone: Home _____ Work _____

U is for Unofficial.

Most everyone knows the Official State of Vermont Flower, Bird, and Insect, but only Real Vermonters know the "real" or Unofficial ones.[1]

Unofficial State Bird	Geesum Crow
Unofficial State Insect	No-see-um[2]
Unofficial State Flower	Cowslip[3]
Unofficial State Tree	White Birch[4]
Unofficial State Coldwater Fish	Brook Trout
Unofficial State Warmwater Fish	Bullhead[5]
Unofficial State Animal	Woodchuck
Unofficial State Song	"I Am a Rock"[6]
Unofficial State Fruit	Road Apples
Unofficial State Vegetable	Fiddlehead Fern
Unofficial State Mineral	Salt
Unofficial State Poet	The Old Squire
Unofficial State Drink	Milk[7]

[1] For all you Flatlanders (and all you Real Vermonters who just want to check up on us), here's the official list: Bird (Hermit Thrush), Insect (Honey Bee), Flower (Red Clover), Tree (Sugar Maple), Coldwater Fish (Brook Trout), Warmwater Fish (Walleye Pike), Animal (Morgan horse), Song (Hail Vermont!). Vermont does not have an Official Fruit, Vegetable, Mineral, or Poet. Robert Frost was named Poet Laureate of Vermont in 1961, however. The official state drink is milk.

[2] They drive Flatlanders nuts.

[3] Cows love to eat red clover. Real Vermonters love to eat cowslips.

[4] Easily overpriced and sold to Flatlanders.

[5] Scares the hell out of trout-fishing Flatlanders.

[6] Someone we know was certain it was "Dead Skunk in the Middle of the Road."

[7] Not goat's milk.

name • address • phone

U

_____
_____
_____ Zip_____
Phone: Home _____ Work _____
_____

_____
_____
_____ Zip_____
Phone: Home _____ Work _____
_____

_____
_____
_____ Zip_____
Phone: Home _____ Work _____
_____

_____
_____
_____ Zip_____
Phone: Home _____ Work _____
_____

_____
_____
_____ Zip_____
Phone: Home _____ Work _____
_____

_____
_____
_____ Zip_____
Phone: Home _____ Work _____
_____

_____
_____ Zip_____
Phone: Home _____ Work _____

V IS FOR VANITY.

name • address • phone

V

_____
_____
_____ Zip_____
Phone: Home _____ Work_____

_____
_____
_____ Zip_____
Phone: Home _____ Work_____

_____
_____
_____ Zip_____
Phone: Home _____ Work_____

_____
_____
_____ Zip_____
Phone: Home _____ Work_____

_____
_____
_____ Zip_____
Phone: Home _____ Work_____

_____
_____
_____ Zip_____
Phone: Home _____ Work_____

_____
_____
_____ Zip_____
Phone: Home _____ Work_____

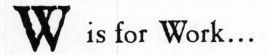
W is for Work...

what Real Vermonters do
between chores.

name • address • phone

_____ Zip_____
Phone: Home _____ Work _____

_____ Zip_____
Phone: Home _____ Work _____

_____ Zip_____
Phone: Home _____ Work _____

_____ Zip_____
Phone: Home _____ Work _____

_____ Zip_____
Phone: Home _____ Work _____

_____ Zip_____
Phone: Home _____ Work _____

_____ Zip_____
Phone: Home _____ Work _____

W   name • address • phone

_____
_____
_____ Zip_____
Phone: Home _____ Work _____
_____
_____
_____ Zip_____
Phone: Home _____ Work _____
_____
_____
_____ Zip_____
Phone: Home _____ Work _____
_____
_____
_____ Zip_____
Phone: Home _____ Work _____
_____
_____
_____ Zip_____
Phone: Home _____ Work _____
_____
_____
_____ Zip_____
Phone: Home _____ Work _____
_____
_____
_____ Zip_____
Phone: Home _____ Work _____

name • address • phone

W

_____
_____
_____ Zip_____
Phone: Home _____ Work _____
_____

_____
_____ Zip_____
Phone: Home _____ Work _____
_____

_____
_____ Zip_____
Phone: Home _____ Work _____
_____

_____
_____ Zip_____
Phone: Home _____ Work _____
_____

_____
_____ Zip_____
Phone: Home _____ Work _____
_____

_____
_____ Zip_____
Phone: Home _____ Work _____
_____

_____
_____ Zip_____
Phone: Home _____ Work _____

X marks the spot.

Through years of diligent research we have located the best spots to find Real Vermonters. They are:

X Alburg Auction House
Alburg

X
Buck and Doe
Island Pond

Cady Commission Sales
Morrisville
X

Golden Gloves Championships
Burlington
X

X Buck's Furniture
Wolcott

X *X* Gaynes Shoppers World
South Burlington

X
Ben Thrasher's Mill
East Barnet

X
Thunder Road
Barre

X
Miller's Store
East Topsham

X
Vermont Book Shop
Middlebury

X
Tunbridge World's Fair
Tunbridge

X
Upper Valley Shopping Plaza
West Lebanon, New Hampshire

X
Wasps Snack Shop
Woodstock

X
Godnick's Fine Furniture
Rutland

X
Calvin Coolidge's Grave
Plymouth

X
Duck Inn Restaurant
Springfield

X
The Taco House
Manchester

X
Grange Hall
West Dummerston

X
Blue Bell Diner
Bennington

X
Halifax

name • address • phone   X

_____
_____
_____ Zip_____
Phone: Home _____ Work _____

_____
_____
_____ Zip_____
Phone: Home _____ Work _____

_____
_____
_____ Zip_____
Phone: Home _____ Work _____

_____
_____
_____ Zip_____
Phone: Home _____ Work _____

_____
_____
_____ Zip_____
Phone: Home _____ Work _____

_____
_____
_____ Zip_____
Phone: Home _____ Work _____

_____
_____
_____ Zip_____
Phone: Home _____ Work _____

Y is for Yarn.

A GOOD BARGAIN

A Real Vermont farmer walked into the local bank and asked to borrow one dollar. Somewhat surprised, his banker said, "Of course."

"And the interest?"

"15 percent."

"Good," said the farmer, "and here's some collateral." It was a $1,000 U. S. Savings Bond. The now doubly mystified officer said it wasn't necessary but agreed to take the bond. The farmer left.

One year later the farmer was back. He stood at the banker's desk and plunked down a dollar, a dime, and a nickel. After the banker gave back the bond, curiosity got the better of him. "Say, Mr. Jones, I don't mean to pry, but would you mind telling me why you wanted to borrow one dollar when you had this $1,000 bond?"

"WELL!" replied Jones, "If I'd put this bond in a safe deposit box, it would have cost me $10.00. This way you charged me only 15 cents!"

name • address • phone

Y

_____

_____

_____ Zip _____
Phone: Home _____ Work _____

_____

_____

_____ Zip _____
Phone: Home _____ Work _____

_____

_____

_____ Zip _____
Phone: Home _____ Work _____

_____

_____

_____ Zip _____
Phone: Home _____ Work _____

_____

_____

_____ Zip _____
Phone: Home _____ Work _____

_____

_____

_____ Zip _____
Phone: Home _____ Work _____

_____

_____

_____ Zip _____
Phone: Home _____ Work _____

Z IS FOR ZIP.

name • address • phone

Z

_____

_____

_____ Zip_____
Phone: Home _____ Work _____

_____

_____

_____ Zip_____
Phone: Home _____ Work _____

_____

_____

_____ Zip_____
Phone: Home _____ Work _____

_____

_____

_____ Zip_____
Phone: Home _____ Work _____

_____

_____

_____ Zip_____
Phone: Home _____ Work _____

_____

_____

_____ Zip_____
Phone: Home _____ Work _____

_____

_____

_____ Zip_____
Phone: Home _____ Work _____

Z

name • address • phone

_____
_____
_____ Zip _____
Phone: Home _____ Work _____
_____

_____
_____
_____ Zip _____
Phone: Home _____ Work _____
_____

_____
_____
_____ Zip _____
Phone: Home _____ Work _____
_____

_____
_____
_____ Zip _____
Phone: Home _____ Work _____
_____

_____
_____
_____ Zip _____
Phone: Home _____ Work _____
_____

_____
_____
_____ Zip _____
Phone: Home _____ Work _____
_____

_____
_____ Zip _____
Phone: Home _____ Work _____